Business Leaders

Google Founders:

▸ Larry Page and Sergey Brin

Business Leaders

Google Founders:

▸ Larry Page and Sergey Brin

Kerrily Sapet

Greensboro, North Carolina

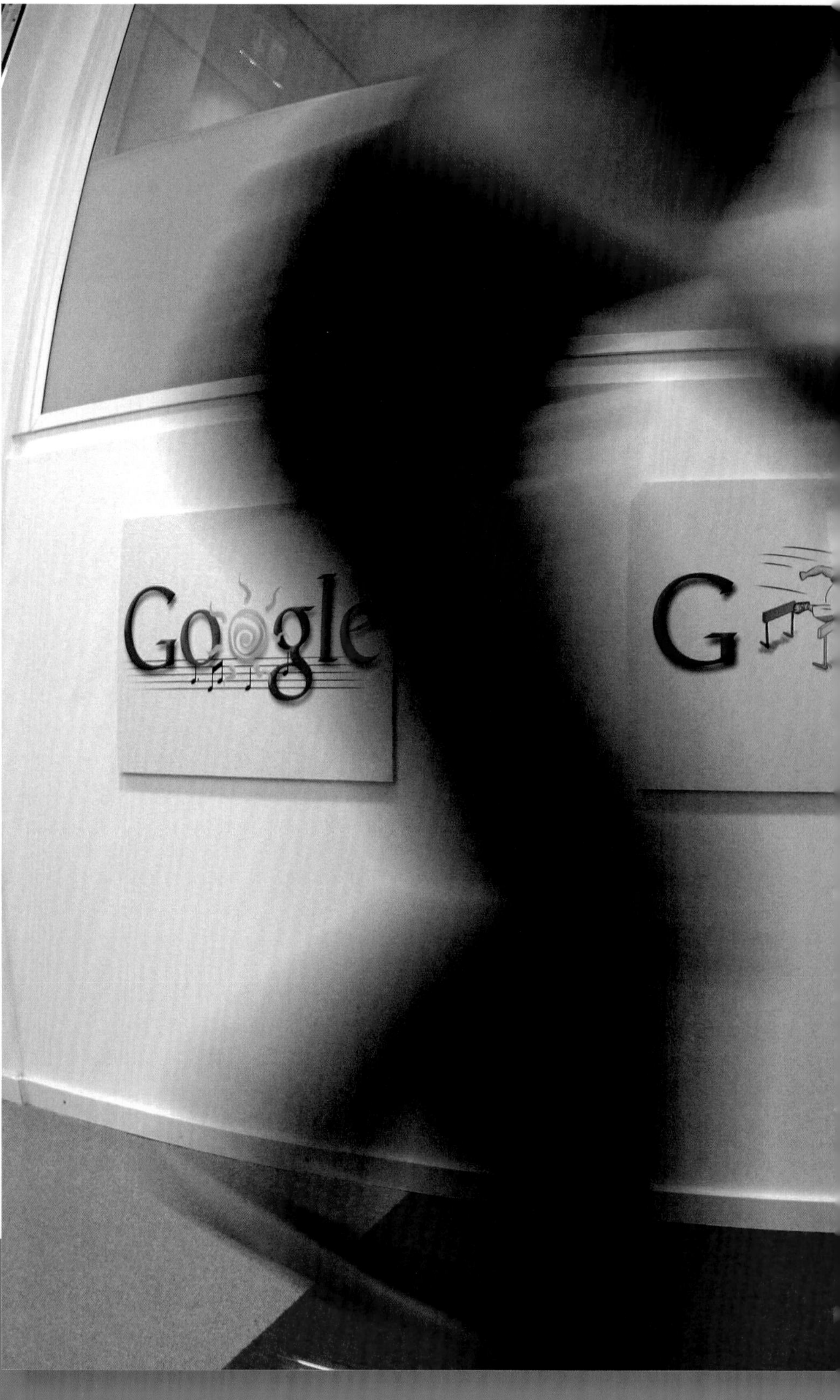
Google

An employee steers his scooter along a corridor of the Google office in Munich, Germany.

Business Leaders
Google Founders: Larry Page and Sergey Brin
Copyright © 2012 by Morgan Reynolds Publishing

Library of Congress Cataloging-in-Publication Data

Sapet, Kerrily.
 Google founders : Larry Page and Sergey Brin / by Kerrily Sapet. -- 1st
ed.
     p. cm. -- (Business leaders)
 Includes bibliographical references and index.
 ISBN 978-1-59935-177-3 (alk. paper) -- ISBN 978-1-59935-213-8
(e-book :
alk. paper)
1. Brin, Sergey, 1973- 2. Page, Larry, 1973- 3. Computer
programmers--United States--Biography 4. Businesspeople--United
States--Biography. 5. Internet programming--United States. 6. Google
(Firm)\ 7. Google. 8. Web search engines. I. Title.
 QA76.2.A2S37 2012
 005.1092--dc23
 [B]
                              2011014665

PRINTED IN THE UNITED STATES OF AMERICA
First Edition

Book cover and interior designed by:
Ed Morgan, navyblue design studio
Greensboro, NC

Table of Contents

Google co-founders Sergey Brin, left, and Larry Page at the company headquarters in Mountain View, California, in 2004

1

The Boys Who Loved Computers

▶ Sergey Brin was born in the drab, concrete landscape of Communist Russia while Larry Page grew up on the green treelined streets of a Michigan university town. It is difficult to imagine two more different beginnings for the founders of Google. However, both boys loved to tinker with computers and to puzzle out complex mathematical problems, and both had academic parents who encouraged their interests. Despite cultural differences, it was their similar intellectual backgrounds that brought them together to create a revolutionary Internet company. One that today places almost limitless information at the fingertips of people around the world.

Google, a search engine, answers more than 1 billion online queries each day, and is available in 117 languages—from Latin to Pig Latin. From students to teachers, actors to CIA agents, athletes to chefs, all turn to Google to answer their questions. Cartoonist Gary Trudeau calls Google "the Swiss Army knife of information retrieval."

With millions of computers running day and night in data centers across the globe, Page and Brin control one of the world's most massive computer systems. Through ground-breaking technology, they have changed the lives of millions of people by providing free, instant access to information, maps, images, and art.

The invention of Google made Larry and Sergey billion-aires. Despite their wealth, they continue to focus on the company they created. To them, Google has more to offer than just information. They plan to use Google as a stepping stone to greater achievements, bettering the world, and improving people's lives.

Before reaching the age of forty, Larry and Sergey accomplished more than most inventors do in a lifetime. Known as the "Google Guys," they hope to develop other technological advancements in areas like medical research and climate change. "I think it [Google] was the smallest of accomplishments that we hope to make over the next twenty years," said Brin.

Lawrence (Larry) Edward Page was born on March 26, 1973 in East Lansing, Michigan. Larry's parents, Carl and Gloria Page, had one other child at the time, nine-year-old Carl Victor Jr. The Pages lived in a middle-class neighborhood near

Michigan State University, where both of Page's parents were professors. Carl taught computer science and Gloria computer programming.

Larry came from a family devoted to education, hard work, and equality. They proudly remembered Larry's grandfather's role in the 1937 Flint Sit-Down Strike, when autoworkers took over a car manufacturing facility in Flint, Michigan, in protest of dangerous working conditions. Larry's father, Carl Victor Page, had survived childhood polio to become the first person in his family to graduate from high school. In 1965, he earned his PhD in computer science from the University of Michigan. Carl was one of the few to hold a degree in the new field.

Larry's foundation in perseverance and dedication also came from his mother's side of the family. Larry's maternal grandfather was Jewish. After immigrating to Israel, he settled in the desert town of Arad near the Dead Sea and eked out a living as a tool and diemaker, despite the scarcity of water and resources.

Beaumont Tower at Michigan State University

Like her husband, Gloria was fascinated by technology. She earned her master's degree in computer science and worked as a database consultant. Larry's parents used computers at home and at work. Inside their house, computer parts and *Popular Science* magazines surrounded Larry.

Five months after Larry's birth, Google's co-founder, Sergey Mikhailovich Brin, was born on August 21, 1973, in Moscow, Russia. Sergey's parents, Mikhail and Eugenia Brin, shared the same passion for technology and education as Page's parents. Mikhail received his PhD in mathematics from Moscow State University. He worked as an economist for Gosplan, a government agency that oversaw economic planning for the Soviet Union. Eugenia, who also held a degree in mathematics, was employed as a civil engineer.

The main building at Moscow State University

The love of numbers ran deep in Sergey's family. He came from a long line of mathematicians and scientists. Sergey's great grandfather had been a math professor in Moscow. His great grandmother had left Russia to study microbiology at the University of Chicago, returning to Moscow in 1921 to help create Russia's Communist framework.

For seventy years, the Communist party ruled the Russian government, industry, and way of life. Communism is an economic system in which the government controls all goods and services. It differs from capitalism, the economic doctrine of the United States, in which citizens can own property and businesses. These differences made the United States and Russia bitter enemies for many years.

Although the Soviet Union seemed prosperous and technologically advanced, these appearances came at the cost of Russian citizens who suffered under the repressive regime. People were forbidden to travel without permission. They couldn't talk freely about the government for fear of being arrested by the KGB, the secret police. Food and other goods were often scarce. A Soviet citizen waited nearly four hundred hours a year in long lines outside stores to purchase items.

Mikhail and Eugenia earned little money and shared a cramped apartment with Sergey's grandmother. A concrete courtyard served as Sergey's playground, where he played for two hours each day, regardless of the weather.

The Brins' religious beliefs worsened their situation. Like Larry's family, they were Jewish. On the streets and at work, they faced harsh anti-Semitism and discrimination. The Communist party banned Jewish people from certain occupations. Mikhail had planned to study astrophysics at

Moscow State University, in hopes of becoming an astronomer. However, officials barred him from the astrophysics program because it shared a university department with nuclear physics. The Soviet government deemed Jewish people too untrustworthy to have access to nuclear secrets. Instead, Mikhail pursued a career in mathematics. The university required him to take entrance examinations specific to Jewish students. Although Mikhail was forbidden to continue his education after graduating, he studied on his own—sneaking into classes and writing research papers. Sergey's mother suffered the same discrimination when she earned her degree in mathematics.

Sergey's parents longed to be free from the oppressive Communist regime. They wanted opportunities for themselves and their son. In 1977, Mikhail attended an international conference, where he met many foreign researchers. When Mikhail returned home, he told his wife they needed to get to America. "He said he wouldn't stay," said Eugenia, "now that he'd seen what life could be about." The Brins applied for visas, documents granting them entry to the United States, in hopes of escaping the Soviet Union. When they submitted their visa applications, Mikhail's employers fired him. Fearing the same retaliation, Eugenia resigned from her job. While officials reviewed their paperwork, Sergey's parents struggled for money, taking temporary jobs wherever they could find work.

Two years later, in 1979, officials granted them their visas. The Brins were lucky to escape; soon after, the Soviet Union closed all emigration. Sergey, his parents, and his grandmother were forced to leave most of their possessions behind when they left their native country. Mikhail explained the journey

The State Historic Museum in Red Square in Moscow

to his son, sadly telling Sergey that the love of one's country isn't always mutual. Six-year-old Sergey would remember the journey as a blur. They traveled from Moscow to Vienna to Paris to America. "We were in different places from day to day," Sergey said.

Upon arriving in the United States, the Brins rented a small cinder block house in the suburbs of Washington, D.C., not far from the University of Maryland. They received support from local Jewish people who had left Russia. "The U.S. was very good to us," Sergey said. "It was a great place, but we started with nothing. We were poor . . . When we first moved to the States we rented a little house, and my parents didn't have a proper room to sleep in. They had to wall off the kitchen. It was a very humble beginning."

A friend of Mikhail's helped him land a teaching position as a math professor at the University of Maryland. Eugenia found work nearby as a scientist at NASA's Goddard Space Flight Center. Sergey began attending a Montessori school. His teachers followed methods developed in the 1920s by Maria Montessori, an Italian physician, who believed children learn by playing. Sergey gravitated to math puzzles, science projects, and maps. He disliked school at first, as he spoke little English and was in a strange country. As Sergey grew accustomed to his new world, he soon excelled and discovered his love of learning.

More than five hundred miles away, in a small university town, six-year-old Larry also attended a Montessori school. For Larry, reading soon became like breathing. On a vacation to Oregon he took an empty suitcase, planning to fill it with books from Powell's Books, a famous store in Portland, Oregon.

In 1979, the year Sergey's family came to the United States, Larry's father obtained an early home computer called the Exidy Sorcerer. Using a homemade typing program, Larry typed entire books on the computer one word at a time. His favorite was the book *Frog and Toad Together*. Not long after, Larry began using the computer for school assignments. None of his teachers had ever seen schoolwork created on a home computer.

In the early 1980s, only eight out of 100 people in the United States had computers in their homes. For many years, computers had functioned solely as calculators. A major breakthrough occurred in 1946 with the Electrical Numerical Integrator and Calculator (ENIAC), nicknamed the "Giant Brain."

The massive machine occupied an entire room and weighed thirty tons. Highly trained operators hooked up cables and flipped the machine's 6,000 switches. The ENIAC performed mathematical calculations at blinding speed; problems previously taking twelve hours to solve were answered in thirty seconds. The U.S. military drove many technological advances, relying on computers to make calculations for the hydrogen bomb and in the space program.

The Electrical Numerical Integrator and Calculator (ENIAC) in Philadelphia, Pennsylvania, circa the late 1940s to early 1950s

In 1976, Steve Wozniak and Steve Jobs, co-founders of the Apple computer company, revolutionized personal computers. Their Apple II became one of the first mass-produced computers. More companies followed and computers rapidly became more advanced and easier to use.

Like many families, the Pages and Brins were excited by the potential offered by the personal computer. Growing up amidst computer parts, Larry especially wanted to figure out how things worked. Armed with a set of screwdrivers, a present from his older brother, Larry dismantled all the power tools around the house. He excelled at taking things apart but often

An Apple II computer

didn't put them back together, aggravating his parents. Soon though, Larry built a working printer—out of Legos.

When Larry was eight years old, his parents divorced. At the same time, his brother left home to study computer science at the University of Michigan. Despite the changes, Larry was still surrounded by family members who loved him and spent time with him. Larry's father especially enjoyed taking his son to Grateful Dead rock concerts.

Larry loved music and played the saxophone. Quiet, shy, and a bit of a loner, he often turned to music, math, and reading. At twelve years old, Larry read a biography about Nikola Tesla, one of the greatest scientific inventors of the late 1800s and early 1900s. The book changed Larry's life and sparked his dream of becoming an inventor.

According to legend, Nikola Tesla was born in Croatia in 1856 at the stroke of midnight during an electrical storm. After immigrating to the United States, Tesla worked for Thomas Edison, quitting after an argument about wages. Tesla focused on his own inventions, working in New York and in Colorado Springs, near the fierce electrical storms common in the Rocky Mountains. His own man-made lightning often surrounded him in his lab.

Despite his brilliance, Tesla led a tragic life. Plagued by obsessive-compulsive disorder, he was a fanatic about cleanliness and about the number three. Tesla circled a block three times before entering a building, used three napkins at meals, and refused to stay in a hotel room unless the room number was divisible by three. By middle age, Tesla's obsessive impulses controlled him. He spent the last years of his life attempting to contact the planet Mars. He died deeply in debt, not receiving recognition for his innovations until years after his death.

Larry quietly absorbed lessons from Tesla's successes and failures, realizing Tesla unwittingly gave away many of his innovations. In the future, Larry would zealously guard his new inventions, keeping them secret until the last moment. "It's a very sad story," Larry said. "I realized Tesla was the greatest inventor, but he didn't accomplish as much as he should have. I realized I wanted to invent things, but I also wanted to change the world. I wanted to get them out there, get them into people's hands so they can use them, because that's what really matters."

As Larry dreamed of inventing, Sergey also discovered his talents. Unlike Larry, he was rebellious and boisterous, and not especially interested in music or reading. "Sergey was a good boy," his father joked, "when he was asleep." Once, on a trip back to Russia, Sergey threw pebbles at a Soviet policeman. His parents had to promise the irate policeman they would severely punish their son at home. The Brins never forgot their reasons for leaving the Soviet Union. Sergey's parents raised their son in the Jewish faith. For a few years, he attended Hebrew school, but he disliked it so much that his parents allowed him to stop going. As an adult, Sergey would choose not to practice his parents' religion. Larry would make the same decision.

Sergey loved to question his teachers and to prove them wrong. They soon recognized his mathematical genius and brought in special teachers to challenge him. "He was a brash young man," said one of Sergey's teachers. "But he was so smart. It just oozed out of him." For Sergey's ninth birthday, his parents bought him a Commodore 64 computer. Sergey began to see ways to apply his skill in math and his scientific mind to computers.

Sergey loved to debate with his parents, who often challenged him more than his teachers. His father was tough and demanding, as a parent and professor. "Almost half the statistics class he taught dropped out after the first session because they couldn't handle his assault and battery on their sense of self," said one student.

When Sergey was nine years old, he overheard his father talking to some colleagues. Mikhail complained that none of his students could solve a complex math problem he assigned. After listening to the conversation, Sergey offered the correct solution to the problem.

The large and clunky Commodore 64 keyboard and mouse

At fifteen years old, and still in high school, Sergey enrolled in math and computer science classes at the University of Maryland. That same year, 1988, his brother Sam was born. Sam soon excelled at basketball and dreamed of becoming a professional athlete. Because the Brins treasured scholarship, Sam grew up believing advanced degrees were necessary for any career. He asked his father, "Is it true that before you play in the NBA you have to get a PhD?" Mikhail answered, "Yes, Sam, that's it."

Sergey graduated from high school a year early and began taking graduate-level classes at the university. At age nineteen, he received his degree from the University of Maryland. After graduation, Sergey joked about running off and joining the circus. He loved gymnastics and had trained on the trapeze for many years. Sergey's path ahead was clear though. He received a National Science Foundation scholarship and soon enrolled at Stanford University to pursue a PhD. Within two years, Larry would join him there.

Like Sergey, Larry excelled in high school. He followed in his family's footsteps and studied computer engineering at the University of Michigan.

The National Science Foundation logo

When Larry used a handheld computer in his classes, no one knew what it was. In Larry's free time, he worked at a doughnut stand and helped the school's solar car team build a car that won a national championship. When Larry graduated in 1995, he too was accepted at Stanford University. Neither he nor Sergey, knew what was in store for them at Stanford.

The arches of the Quad at Stanford University

2

"LarryandSergey"

▶As soon as he set foot on Stanford University's campus in 1995, Larry Page met Sergey Brin. Brin served as a tour guide, walking Page and other new graduate students around Stanford's sprawling campus.

Located between San Francisco and San Jose, California, Stanford's campus is fringed with palm trees and eucalyptus. Students attend classes in rectangular cream-colored buildings, lined with arches and topped with red-tiled roofs, in classic Spanish style. More than seventy sculptures dot the neatly trimmed green lawns. Some of the 15,000 students enjoy fountain hopping, leaping into the blue waters of the many fountains on campus, and steam tunneling, exploring the university's underground steam tunnels.

More than just the beautiful, sunny campus attracted Page and Brin to Stanford. They were lured by the school's reputation. Since the school opened in 1891, it has evolved into one of the world's top universities, recognized for its excellence in science, technology, and math. Stanford is home to scholars who have won Nobel and Pulitzer Prizes and Presidential Medals of Freedom. Stanford graduates founded Yahoo! and Hewlett-Packard, a leading technology company.

The chance to take part in cutting-edge computer science research excited both Page and Brin. However, when the future co-founders met that day, they argued nonstop about random issues. "We both found each other obnoxious," said Brin. "But we say it a little bit jokingly. Obviously we spent a lot of time talking to each other, so there was something there. We had a kind of bantering thing going."

Brin and Page differed in personality. Confident and social, Brin was spontaneous and intense. Page was a shy midwesterner who worried about being sent home for not meeting the school's rigorous standards. "They were both brilliant, some of the smartest people I have ever met," said Stanford professor Rajeev Motwani. "But they were brilliant in different ways. . . . If there was a group meeting of twenty people, Sergey was holding court. You wouldn't notice [Larry] if he was in a crowd, but then afterward he would say, 'Hey, what do you think of this idea?'"

Despite their initial squabbling, Page and Brin had more similarities than differences. Math and science framed their respective childhoods. Soon they became nearly inseparable. Friends called them "LarryandSergey." As they delved into research projects together, each brought different abilities to their work. They were like "two swords sharpening each other," said one professor.

As Brin had already mastered graduate-level coursework at the University of Maryland, he aced all ten of Stanford's required doctoral exams on the first try. Most students didn't pass all of the exams until their third year. Brin didn't need to take any classes to earn his PhD; his remaining requirement was to write his thesis.

Brin explored many subjects at Stanford. "I expected him to get his PhD and to become somebody, maybe a professor," said Brin's father. "I asked him if he was taking any advanced courses one semester. He said, 'Yes, advanced swimming.'" Brin studied everything from genetics and molecular biology—the make up of molecules in living cells—to developing an individualized online movie rating system. "I tried so many different things in grad school," he said. "The more you stumble around, the more likely you are to stumble across something valuable."

Page's first year at Stanford was rough. Not long after he settled into life on campus, his father became critically ill. Carl Page suffered from complications following pneumonia. His health declined rapidly, and his ability to breathe deteriorated. Within weeks, at only fifty-eight years old, Carl passed away. He would be remembered as a pioneering scholar and teacher who loved a heated debate. Carl Page's sudden death left a hole in his son's life. Fortunately, Larry's brother, Carl Jr., lived and worked near Stanford. The two brothers shared memories of their father and supported each other during the difficult time.

Despite the traumatic loss, Page continued his studies, burying himself in his work. At the time, Silicon Valley was buzzing about Netscape, a technical start-up company with a product called a browser. Browsers enable users to navigate the Internet. Founded only sixteen months before, the company had swiftly become worth more than $3 billion. Wall Street investors grew hungry to finance other cutting-edge Internet companies in hopes of getting rich fast. Netscape's success launched an Internet era in Silicon Valley.

Situated south of San Francisco Bay's choppy waters, Silicon Valley is framed by the sun-baked rolling mountains of the Diablo Range and the ancient redwoods of the Santa Cruz Mountains. Until the 1940s, sprawling orchards, filled with peaches, lemons, apricots, and almonds, blanketed the valley. During World War II, the U.S. Navy located a research facility in the area. Other technology firms soon followed.

Journalist Don Hoefler coined the term "Silicon Valley" in 1972. At the time, many of the companies in the valley were researching semiconductors, a component of electrical devices. Most semiconductors are created with silicon, a common element contained in sand and quartz. The name stuck. Today, hundreds of high-tech companies, such as Apple, Yahoo!, and

A view of Silicon Valley. The southern tip of San Francisco Bay is just out of sight around the knoll to the right.

eBay make Silicon Valley their home. The valley has more millionaires per capita than anywhere else in the United States.

Stanford University's nearby science and engineering schools serve as incubators for the region's high-tech companies. The environment fosters student entrepreneurs to develop commercial projects spun out from university research. The Internet boom in the 1990s made it difficult to stay in school; Stanford students often received lucrative job offers. But Page and Brin weren't looking to get rich. Instead they devoted themselves to their research.

In January of 1996, Stanford's computer science students and faculty moved into a new four-story building with the words William Gates Computer Science chiseled on the front. Although Bill Gates, co-founder of the Microsoft Corporation, hadn't attended Stanford, he donated $6 million towards the construction of the building. Microsoft hired many Stanford graduates, and Gates hoped to help entice new talent to his company.

Page and four other graduate students set up an office in Gates 360. Although Brin had another office, he spent long hours in Gates 360. The office became home for all of them. The students often stayed up late, studying and debating technology. They once argued whether it was possible to assemble a building-size structure entirely out of lima beans. Technology ruled the office. A bucket of water with a computer-controlled pump watered the plants that climbed to the ceiling. A piano plugged into a computer provided music. A computer rack made out of Legos stood in one corner. Both Page and Brin loved to build with Legos. Years later, Brin would even fiddle with Legos during an interview, jokingly telling the reporter, "I was hoping to build a Lego nuclear reactor, but I think I have a bazooka-wielding robot."

From Gates 360, Brin and Page carried out their research. Brin focused mainly on data mining, the idea of extracting information from mountains of random data. Brin wanted to apply data mining technology to the Internet, organizing large amounts of information to make searches more efficient.

As the Internet had emerged in the 1990s, it impacted communication just as the telegraph and telephone had in their times. In the 1950s, the U.S. government had spearheaded the development of the

Legos gave Brin and Page much needed breaks.

Internet by creating a research agency called ARPA. ARPA's goal was to develop a technological edge over Russia and strengthen America's communications systems in the event of a Soviet nuclear strike. ARPA aimed to bring together the brainpower at universities across the United States through a network of connected computers used to share scientific and academic information. By 1969, researchers had linked computers between Stanford and the University of California, Los Angeles. Today, millions of computers are connected in a global network, with billions of Internet users.

The World Wide Web is the interconnected Web of information on the Internet, in which billions of pages link to each other. From 1993 to 1996, the number of Web sites on the Internet increased from 130 to 600,000. People also began communicating by electronic mail, or e-mail. The Internet provided massive amounts of information, in a disorganized clutter of Web sites. Searches—or queries—yielded hundreds or thousands of results in no particular order. People could spend hours sifting through a maze of sites to find the information they needed. "Search was not pretty in those days," said Stanford's Motwani. "You'd get a slew of results that were completely meaningless."

As Brin researched data mining, Page studied the search engine AltaVista. A search engine is a software program designed to locate items on the Internet. Page noticed the search results included links that highlighted words from the query. The creator of a Web site often provides links to other sites that offer valuable, related information. Computer users wanting to learn more click on a link that takes them to a different Web page. To Page, the essence of the Web was the links joining pages to each other. When Page visited a site, he could see the backlinks, or sites linking it to others. He realized that the number of backlinks offered a way to rank sites.

Page wanted a big database in order to do more research on backlinks. He decided to download the entire World Wide Web onto his computer. Others scoffed at the idea. But to Brin, with his interest in data mining, the idea made sense.

Page and Brin teamed up to download the Web and analyze links. They created a computer program called a crawler or spider. A spider crawls the Web, retrieving Web pages and documents. It visits Web sites, summarizes their content, and feeds the information into a program that creates an index of Web pages. When a user types a query, the search engine consults the index and returns results in a list of Web pages with links to those terms. Page and Brin's crawler ran nonstop, continuously updating the index. The two students worked long hours, often until five in the morning, stopping only to dine on the five dollar student special buffet at a small restaurant nearby.

As Page studied backlinks, he decided not all links were equal. They reminded him of notes in research papers. One way to measure the importance of a research article is to count the number of studies referring to it. The more useful and important the article, the more it is cited. Similarly, on the Web, the more useful Web sites had more backlinks.

10,000,000,000,000,000,000,000,000,000,000,
000,000,000,000,000,000,000,000,000,000

Brin devised an algorithm, or formula with a series of steps solving a problem, involving more than 500 million variables. The formula assigned a value to each site, taking into account the number of backlinks. The results were neutral, not swayed by advertising, but by how useful others found the site.

Page and Brin called their new technology PageRank, as a tribute to its function and founder. Using a search engine and PageRank, users could search the Internet for information and get results prioritized by relevance and importance. Other search engines just matched words in a query; PageRank offered results in a logical manner. "The perfect search engine would understand exactly what you mean and give back exactly what you want," said Page.

Page and Brin developed a search engine to accompany PageRank. At first they called it BackRub because it used backlinks. Their logo became Page's left hand, scanned and converted to black and white. They made the search engine available to students at Stanford.

Soon, Page and Brin decided to rename BackRub. They brainstormed for days and considered calling it Whatbox. Their officemate, Sean Anderson, suggested *Googolplex*, meaning a company that allows people to search vast amounts of data. Googol is the number one followed by one hundred zeros. Page and Brin liked the sound of it and the immense amount of information the word represented. They shortened it to *googol*.

A googol is the number one followed by one hundred zeros.

000,000,000,000,000,000,000,000,
000,000,000,000,000,000,000,000

"We were confused about how to spell this, and so we actually spelled it incorrectly," said Page. "It is a mathematical term and it is spelled g-o-o-g-o-l. So that is the right way Google is spelled." Brin and Page liked their misspelling though and registered Google as their domain name or Web address.

In August 1996, Page and Brin released the first version of Google on Stanford's Web site, making it available for students and faculty. Soon Google had hundreds of satisfied users. Its popularity spread by word of mouth. Within months, Google was at maximum capacity, handling 10,000 searches a day from Stanford. The system required an enormous amount of memory. Instead of using one megacomputer to store data, Page and Brin linked smaller computers to their network. Still, it wasn't enough. "We sat around the room and looked at the machines and said, 'This is about how many searches we can do, and we need more computers.' Our whole history has been like that," said Page. "We always need more computers."

Short on cash, Page and Brin scrounged for computers at the university's receiving dock where packages arrived. When they saw someone take a delivery of twenty computers, they asked for a spare. They "snarfed a whole bunch of machines of all different types," said Brin. They also bought parts and built their own machines, assembling and stringing together inexpensive personal computers, or PCs. Page and Brin spent $15,000 of their own money, using three credit cards, to buy hard drives that could store a terabyte of data. They crammed the computers into Gates 360—their data center.

Despite Google's success, Page and Brin wanted to finish their PhDs. They decided to try to sell their PageRank technology. In March 1998, at a Chinese restaurant in Palo

Alto, they met Paul Flaherty, the architect of AltaVista. More than half of the people searching the Internet used AltaVista. Although people considered it one of the best search engines, it didn't rank information. Page and Brin explained to Flaherty how Google was better than AltaVista. "They were excited by what they were able to do," said Dennis Allison, the Stanford professor who arranged the meeting. "They were very anxious to share it. They were basically saying in a polite way, 'AltaVista is dead meat. It doesn't do what is needed.' These guys had a PageRank." Page and Brin offered to sell PageRank to Flaherty for $1 million. Flaherty declined their offer, as did other companies. Nobody wanted to buy search technology. Companies wanted users to come to their sites to shop and spend money, not just ask questions.

Page and Brin realized they had hit a wall. Without more funding, they couldn't buy the computer parts they needed to keep expanding Google. David Filo, the Stanford student who co-founded Yahoo!, advised Page and Brin to start their own business.

One of their professors, David Cheriton, knew Andy Bechtolsheim, a legendary investor in successful start-up companies. Cheriton suggested Bechtolsheim meet Page and Brin to discuss Google. Although the two students disliked getting up early, Cheriton arranged the appointment for eight in the morning

David Filo, co-founder of Yahoo!

on his front porch, which Bechtolsheim passed each morning on his way to work.

At their meeting, Page and Brin told Bechtolsheim how they could download, index, and rapidly search the Internet, using a network of inexpensive personal computers. They explained that they needed money to buy more machines. Bechtolsheim realized Page and Brin's idea solved a real problem. He liked that they didn't plan to waste money on advertising or expensive equipment. "Other Web sites took a good chunk of venture funding and spent it on advertising," Bechtolsheim said. "They [Page and Brin] believed in word of mouth. This was the opposite approach. Build something of value and deliver a service compelling enough that people would just use it."

Bechtolsheim told the pair it was one of the best ideas he'd heard in years and wrote them a check for $100,000, twice the amount they had suggested. He made the check out to Google, Inc., a company that didn't exist yet. Afterwards, Page and Brin celebrated by going to Burger King.

Back in Page's dorm room, Page and Brin put Bechtolsheim's check in a desk drawer—because there was no business named Google, Inc. They had no company bank account and no place to deposit the money. The two of them filled out the legal paperwork to create their company. On September 7, 1998, Google, Inc. became an official company.

Too busy with their new company to continue their graduate studies, Page and Brin took leaves of absence from Stanford. The decision made their parents unhappy. "We were definitely upset," said Brin's mother. "We thought everybody in their right mind ought to get a PhD." With grim looks on their faces,

Page and Brin took empty boxes into Gates 360. They left with full boxes that contained the remnants of their lives as graduate students. Page and Brin were now business owners, unsure whether their path ahead held success or failure.

The house where Google co-founders Larry Page and Sergey Brin
first set up shop in Menlo Park, California

3

| From Garage to Googleplex |

▶After launching Google, Page and Brin set up business in a small garage in Menlo Park, close to Palo Alto. For $1,700 a month, they rented a few rooms and the garage, where they kept their computers and gadgets. Page and Brin flipped a coin to decide who would be Google's president. Brin won. Page became chief executive officer, or CEO. They hired their first employee, Craig Silverstein, a friend and fellow Stanford graduate student.

Their sparse office hardly looked like that of a successful company. Page, Brin, and Silverstein sat at desks made from old pine doors propped up on sawhorses. A few rickety tables and chairs, a decrepit washer and dryer, and a tiny refrigerator rested on top of the worn turquoise shag carpet. Page and Brin worked in the garage nearly twenty-four hours a day. They were driven but knew little about running a company.

The sum of their business experience was the few months Page had worked at a doughnut stand.

Successful companies often have humble beginnings. That year, a journalist asked Bill Gates about the biggest threats Microsoft faced. Instead of listing well-known adversaries, like Apple or Netscape, Gates responded, "I fear someone in a garage who is devising something completely new." Innovative new companies, such as Google, could grow up to challenge established companies like Microsoft. Page and Brin certainly had big plans. By the doorbell of their apartment, they taped up the handwritten sign *Google's World Headquarters.*

Bill Gates in 2004

Through a friend, Page and Brin met Ruth Kedar, a graphic designer and assistant professor at Stanford. They decided to hire her to design Google's logo. They wanted something basic, but playful, representing the values of their company. "It was important for them to tell me about themselves, what they believe in, where they see themselves in the future . . . ," Kedar said. "At the time, many people were afraid to use the Internet, and it was important to broadcast something user-friendly both on the home page and in the logo. Something simple, that you didn't need to be scared of, something catchy and full of life."

Kedar presented several sketches to Page and Brin. In one drawing, Google's o's looked like magnifying glasses; in another, they looked like a target. After many revisions, she settled on the typeface "Catull" to write the word Google in colorful letters, with slightly tilted o's, on a white background. The uncluttered logo remains in place today, representing simple, free Internet searching.

Page and Brin fanatically kept the number of words on their homepage to a minimum, just twenty-eight words, so it looked clean and quick to read at a glance. Nothing about Google was slow. At the click of a mouse, a query was sent to Google's machines and compared with all the documents stored in the index. In a quarter of a second (an eyeblink is one-tenth of a second), the system prepared a list of the most relevant pages.

By the end of their first year in business, Page and Brin were attracting attention. In December, *PC Magazine* listed Google.com as one of the Top 100 Web sites for 1998. Making the list put Google on the radar for thousands of people. Other companies were focusing less on search and more on providing all-purpose sites. These changes drove people to Google's free, quality search.

As Google's popularity spread by word of mouth, the number of searches soared. Google was now receiving 500,000 queries a day. Page and Brin struggled to keep up with demand. They had eight employees, and soon hired more, one of whom brought Google's first company dog, Yoshka, to work. In need of more computers, they began ordering them in packs of twenty-one.

After only five months of working out of the garage, Page and Brin ran out of room. In early 1999, they rented an office above a bike shop in downtown Palo Alto. They stocked their office with plenty of coffee, coolers of fruit juice, and chewy red Swedish Fish candies. They used their ping-pong table as a conference table and kept hockey sticks and Rollerblades on hand, for when they took rare breaks.

Swedish Fish candies

Page and Brin wanted their company to have a creative, free-spirit atmosphere. "To just invent something and have a great idea is a lot of work, but it is not enough," said Page. "You have to get it out in the world. At Google, it is a combination of scientific skills, and mathematical skills, and computer skills, and also very strong skills about how to get people excited about their work." The pair wrote a list of reasons to work for Google, like cool technology, free snacks and drinks, and shares of stock. Start-up companies offer stock, or shares in the company, to their employees. In the future, if the company is successful, employees can sell their stock and make money.

To keep Google up and running, Page and Brin needed more money. Nearby Sand Hill Road in Menlo Park was home to many venture capital firms that invest money in start-up companies in exchange for stock. They take high risks by investing in the early stages of a company, in hopes of big returns and financial success.

Page and Brin made appointments at several of the venture capital firms. They needed money but didn't want to relinquish any control of Google in exchange for it. The duo had difficulty persuading serious investors to fund a company that only offered search services.

After several rejections, Page and Brin met with venture capitalists John Doerr and Michael Moritz. Unlike other investors, Doerr and Moritz were intrigued. They liked Page and Brin as a team and realized a company like Google had the potential to grow and change as the Internet evolved.

Both Doerr and Moritz decided to take a chance on Google. However, they refused to invest jointly, not wanting to cede any control to the other. Although Page and Brin needed money quickly to keep Google in business, they boldly told Doerr and Moritz they would walk away if the two investors couldn't reach a compromise. Within days, the four of them ironed out the details of the deal. Both financiers agreed to invest $12.5 million each in Google, with the requirement that Page and Brin hire an expert executive to help transform Google into a profitable business.

Soon after the investment deal, Page and Brin took a much needed vacation and attended the Burning Man Festival in Nevada's Black Rock Desert. During the weeklong festival, people flock to a constructed town of tents and campsites in the middle of the desert. With no food or water available, participants bring all their supplies. The free artistic and social gathering is symbolized by a tall wooden figure of a man, that is burned at the end of the week. Before Page and Brin left, Google employee Dennis Hwang created a doodle on Google's homepage logo. The drawing of a stick man in the second letter *o* told Google users Page and Brin would be at the Burning Man Festival. The famous Google Doodle was born.

Not long after, Brin created a Halloween logo on Google's homepage with two pumpkins over the letter *o's*. Google users loved the designs. Page and Brin began to feature a few artistic doodles each month, celebrating holidays and events such as New Year's Day and the Olympics. Soon the list expanded. Google Doodles have commemorated the birthdays of artists, entertainers, and scientists, and paid tributes to important events like the Wright Brothers' first flight and Martin Luther King Jr. Day.

The Google home page celebrating Jane Austen's 235th birthday

With the money to expand the company, Page and Brin decided Google needed additional computers and memory.

They ordered computers in eighty packs from online companies. They also visited Fry's, a chain of large electronics stores. Page and Brin stocked up, returned to their office, and began to rip the computers apart, removing any parts that ate up power. They rebuilt the machines, creating streamlined computers strung together with custom software and wiring. The computers, dubbed *Googleware*, were "garden-variety PCs on steroids," said one author. For every one dollar Page and Brin spent, they averaged three times more computer power and memory than their competitors.

However, Google's computers burned out within one or two years, due to the use they received. Several machines died each day. Page and Brin used enough computers that if one cluster went down, other computers, that shared copies of the Internet and data, automatically took over.

Page and Brin spread data and tasks over a vast number of computers in multiple locations so the entire system could handle problems without crashing. They ran three off-site data centers—two in California and one in Washington, D.C.—and soon added more across the country, all monitored from a single location. The computers were housed in chilled warehouses to prevent the equipment from overheating. The warehouse companies charged by the foot of space used, so Page and Brin crammed as many machines as possible on top of each other on refrigerator-sized racks. A fire at one of their data centers put Google's computer system to the test. Although it took six fire trucks to control the blaze, most Google users never even knew there was a problem.

Google's first production server. Pulled back "hair" (cords) reveals a rack of cheap networked PCs.

One day Page and Brin would have hundreds of thousands of custom-built machines. "They run the largest computer system in the world," said Stanford president John Hennessy. "I don't think there is even anything close."

Page and Brin, now nicknamed the Google Guys, found they had outgrown their offices again. They decided to lease the second floor of a building in the town of Mountain View, a ten-minute bike ride from Stanford. Soon they expanded to the first floor. Next, they leased the building next door. People called it the Googleplex.

The culture inside the Googleplex reflected Page's and Brin's personalities, with gadgets, foosball tables, lava lamps, espresso machines, and large exercise balls and beanbags as chairs. Because employees worked long hours each day, Page and Brin tried to make their working atmosphere pleasant and convenient. They started an on-site laundry service and chartered buses with wireless Internet, so their employees could work during their commutes from nearby San Francisco.

In November of 1999, Page and Brin decided to hire a chef for a company cafeteria. They held a cook-off, won by Charlie Ayers, a former chef for the Grateful Dead. Soon Google employees, or Googlers, dined on foods like sushi, sweet potato jalapeno soup, and chocolate fondue. Page and Brin instituted Seafood Fridays with a smorgasbord of seafood—from oysters to lobster.

People recognized that Google wasn't an average company, and Page and Brin weren't typical business owners. Young and enthusiastic, they made information free and accessible for everyone. Google stood in stark contrast to other big companies like Microsoft. In 2000, Microsoft violated anti-trust

Larry Page, left, and Sergey Brin, rest on
bean bags at Google's headquarters in 2000.

laws, or laws that prohibit unfair business practices. The trial, which Microsoft lost, depicted Bill Gates as the head of a corporate monster. Google benefited from the negative publicity Microsoft received. "Competition is a good thing," Gates responded. "On the other hand, nobody's doing a very good job of competing with Google right now."

Soon, Google was named the leading Internet search engine, with 99 percent of users ranking it better than its competition. Page and Brin began translating their site into other languages. They started up Web sites in France, Germany, Denmark, Portugal, and other European countries. As Google continued to expand and hire new employees, nicknamed Nooglers, other Internet companies collapsed.

For many years, investors had been pouring money into Internet start-up companies. A mania for Internet stocks caused prices to rise to an all-time high on NASDAQ, the electronic stock market where shares in most Internet companies are traded. In 2000, 457 private Internet companies became public companies by allowing investors to buy their stock. Many of the companies doubled in value on the first day. People called it the "dot com bubble," as the phrase .com was a suffix in many Web sites' names. However, investors soon realized that few of these businesses had plans for making money. Most had been financed by venture capitalists. The companies gave away services, in hopes of building a customer base, while figuring out ways to make money from their users. Although some of the businesses did become successful, many failed. In March 2000, the bubble burst and Internet stocks plummeted in value. High-tech firms across Silicon Valley went bankrupt.

Google resembled the failing Internet companies in some ways. They too existed on venture capital funds and provided free services, without generating revenue. However, being a private company, not controlled by the stock market, helped Google stay afloat as others sank around them. Page and Brin held the reins to one of the only Internet companies hiring in the wake of the stock market crash. They attracted many of the bright individuals who had recently lost their jobs.

The press raved about Page and Brin's company. Google was free, easy to use, and practical. Users appreciated the site's creativity and humor. Page and Brin soon started another Google yearly tradition of issuing an April Fool's Day joke. In 2000, Page and Brin told the site's users to try MentalPlex, a faster way to search. They advised users to peer into a swirling circle on the screen, project a mental image of what they wanted to search, and visualize clicking the circle. Google's followers loved it. Another year Page and Brin announced a free Internet service called TiSP, the Toilet Internet Service Provider, suggesting people obtain a connection by flushing one end of a fiber optic cable down the toilet. Page and Brin also began hiding little jokes, called Easter eggs, on their site. During the World Cup in 2000, when users entered soccer-related search terms, Google's homepage changed to read "Gooo....al!" instead of Google.

That year, Google won its first Webby Award. The Webby Awards are the Oscars of the Internet. Just as the Oscars, or Academy Awards, honor the finest actors and films of the year, the Webby Awards recognize the best of the Internet.

Started in 1996, the Webby Awards are presented by the International Academy of Digital Arts and Sciences, whose members include Web and business experts, writers, and talented artists. There are four awards categories: Web sites, interactive advertising, online film and video, and mobile and apps. Each category has two honors: the Webby Award—selected by the Academy—and the People's Voice Award—selected by online voters. The Academy receives tens of thousands of entries from countries around the world. Winners have included eBay, Wikipedia, and Amazon.com.

In 2000, the Webby Awards were held at the Masonic Center in San Francisco's posh Nob Hill neighborhood. Inside the large, modern auditorium, Google swept the Technical Achievements category, winning the Webby Award and the People's Voice Award as voted by 134,000 users. Google's team members accepted the award by skating onto the stage on roller skates and wearing Google hockey jerseys. Webby winners are limited to acceptance speeches of five words or less. "We love you, Google users," said Brin. In Google's press release, Brin continued his speech. "We want to thank all our loyal Google fans who voted for us," he said. "They are the most fun and spirited in all of cyberspace. Their continued support and enthusiasm has helped to fuel Google's phenomenal month over month traffic growth."

In just two years, Page and Brin's company had become the largest, fastest search engine in the world, with more than 1 billion Web pages in its index. "Google's new gigantic index means that you can search the equivalent of a stack of paper more than 70 miles high in less than half a second," said Page. "This unprecedented power enables millions of Google users worldwide to communicate, learn and entertain like never before."

With their success, Page and Brin faced critical questions. Their operating costs now exceeded $500,000 a month, rapidly devouring their venture capital funds. Their expenses mounted with their need to meet rising user demand. Page and Brin realized once again that they needed more money and more computers. The Google Guys had to figure out how to make money before they ran out of it.

Jobs

Google Search

Search: ⊙ the we

More and more people started using Google to search the Web.

4

▶ By 2000, Page and Brin struggled to keep up with the costs of running a business on Google's scale. Some people figured that the Google Guys would start charging their hooked users to search Google's massive index. But Page and Brin liked offering Google for free and planned to keep it that way.

Many Internet sites depended on advertising. Yahoo!, which primarily served as a home to registered e-mail users, contracted out search services to the company Overture, Inc. Overture made money selling ads to accompany search results, guaranteeing advertisers their businesses would be included more frequently if they paid extra.

Neither Page nor Brin liked the idea of advertising on Google. Instead they had focused on licensing their search technology to others. However, with the crunch to stay in business, they decided to sell ad space on Google.

To make it clear that advertising didn't impact the results of the search, Page and Brin kept Google's homepage free of ads and instituted strict guidelines. All ads were brief and identical in appearance. Each contained a headline, a two-sentence description, and a link to the site. They didn't permit pop up ads or flashing graphics. A vertical line separated the search results from the ads, which appeared to the right of the screen and were clearly labeled *sponsored links*.

The queries Google users entered triggered certain ads. If a person typed in the word *guitar*, Google returned search results along with a list of sponsored links related to guitars. Just as PageRank listed sites in relevant order, Google's ads functioned the same way. Page and Brin ranked ads, not by which advertiser spent the most money, but by how frequently users clicked on those ads. Popular ads rose to the top of the sponsored links results.

In October 2000, Page and Brin launched AdWords, their self-service advertising program. Advertisers signed up online, activating their account with a credit card. Ads could be up and running within minutes. The system cut costs for Google, and gave all businesses—small and large—equal opportunities to place ads.

Using an automated, online system, advertisers made bids to have their ads appear next to specific search terms. For example, the swimwear company Speedo might bid to run ads next to the keywords *swimsuit* or *goggles*. Page and Brin set the minimum bid at five cents. Companies spent anywhere from ten dollars to thousands of dollars in auctions.

Page and Brin's AdWords program revolutionized online advertising. In the science of marketing, companies study how to target ads to the people most likely to buy their products. For many years, advertisers just bought space on billboards, in newspapers and magazines, and on television. Now, more businesses were marketing their products and services to online users. AdWords gave advertisers instant access to users who were matching themselves to ads by going online and typing in search terms.

AdWords solved the mystery of how Page and Brin could make money from searches. The small, targeted text ads soon turned Google into a moneymaking machine. Page and Brin were operating a twenty-four-hour advertising store, in which thousands of keywords and phrases could be sold.

Although Google was becoming an incredibly successful company, the two men running it, both still in their twenties, had minimal business experience. When Page and Brin received their funding, Doerr and Moritz had stipulated they hire an experienced executive to help run Google. Not wanting to give up any control of their company, Page and Brin had found excuses to reject each candidate Doerr and Moritz proposed. They met with about fifteen candidates who were invited to join Page and Brin for a meal in the cafeteria and to attend staff meetings. "They thought everyone they had talked to was a clown," said one Google employee. "The candidates didn't understand technology." But Google's investors insisted on "day-to-day adult supervision" and threatened to revoke their $25 million in funding.

In March 2001, Page and Brin met with candidate Eric Emerson Schmidt. With a PhD in computer science, Schmidt had the technical background Page and Brin required. Schmidt also possessed the experience Google's investors wanted,

Eric Schmidt in 2005

having held top positions at multinational computer companies, such as Sun Microsystems. When Page and Brin sat down with Schmidt, they peppered him with questions and argued with him. The Google Guys respected Schmidt's ability to hold his own in the debate and agreed to hire him as their chief executive officer. Titles switched. Page became the president of products and Brin, the president of technology. Doerr and Moritz realized Page and Brin had made the right decision by waiting. "They resisted hiring ordinary people, and that's a wonderful tribute to them," said Moritz. "One of the many lessons I learned from the Google investment is the importance of hiring spectacular people. Sometimes it frustrated us, but they were spot on."

Schmidt worked on improving Google's financial record keeping, payroll systems, and business dealings. Page and Brin had been using Quicken, a personal finance software program unequipped to handle a company with two hundred employees and large amounts of advertising revenue. Although Page and Brin played practical jokes on Schmidt at first, they came to value his experience.

For the first time in the span of Google's existence, Page and Brin turned a profit. Due to AdWords, by the end of 2001 Google had made $7 million. Although the program started with only 350 advertisers, big name companies like Walmart, one of America's largest retailers, had begun advertising on Google. Although more than half of Google's searches came from users outside of the United States, only 5 percent of the ads originated in other countries. Page and Brin opened offices in London, Hamburg, Tokyo, and Toronto. Google now had more than 3 billion Web pages in its index and offered search services in sixty-six languages, including invented languages such as Klingon.

With the increase in profit, Page and Brin had the time and resources to devote to inventing other Google services. They soon launched Google Images, a searchable database containing approximately 250 million images and photographs. Google Images became an instant hit; nothing else like it existed. Page and Brin also introduced Google Maps. Users could view interactive maps, based on satellite imagery, and get detailed directions between destinations. A hidden joke on the site instructed people to *kayak across the Pacific Ocean* when they asked for directions to a location near a body of water.

The World Trade Center during the attacks on September 11, 2001

Eventually, Page and Brin would take Google Images further, offering over 1.2 billion images. They would also launch Google Earth, giving users the capability to see three-dimensional images of any place on the planet and the moon. Using satellite imagery, people could locate and zoom in on their neighborhoods and houses, even seeing the cars in their driveways and pools in their backyards.

Another Google service, Google News, soon debuted. Google News supplied links to articles from 4,000 news sources around the world. Users found Google News especially helpful the year it debuted. After a series of terrorist attacks on September 11, 2001, many people went online for news. They searched for information about the World Trade Center, the buildings in New York City demolished by suicide bombers; Al Qaeda, the terrorist network that carried out the attacks; and its leader Osama Bin Laden. In the days following September 11, Google News provided an important service to worried people at a time when news sites were overwhelmed by online traffic.

In 2002, Page and Brin increased their business even more by contracting their search services to Internet sites like Yahoo! and AOL. Now, millions of subscribers to those sites saw a small search box on every page, stating the search was powered by Google. Soon, more than 25,000 sites had Google search boxes. Page and Brin also expanded their company by acquiring the site Blogger.com, a Web log, or blog, hosting company.

Not long after, Page and Brin introduced another advertising program, AdSense, that matched advertisers with Web sites. With a new modification, called cost-per-click, Google's

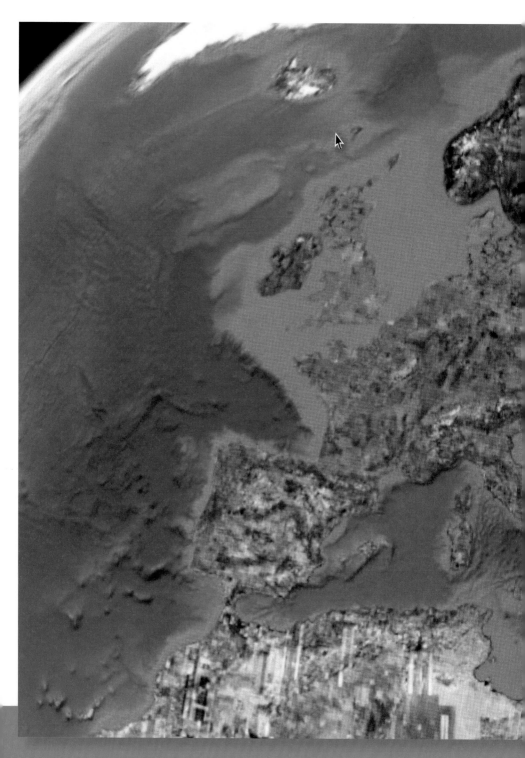

Europe as seen on Google Earth

program only charged advertisers when users clicked on their ads. By 2002, Google was generating $440 million in sales and earning $100 million in profits.

Google's growth stunned people. According to Deloitte Touche Tohmatsu, an international financial organization, in its first five years Google grew faster than any company in history. The American Dialect Society ranked the word google the most useful word of 2003.

Page and Brin now had more than 1,600 employees. Thousands of resumes streamed in each week. Page and Brin worried Google was growing so rapidly they would lose the company's culture. They decided to write a statement defining Google's core beliefs. Page and Brin assembled a group of longtime employees. They gathered in the cafeteria and spent hours jotting down ideas, like *Don't be late*, *Don't lose user focus*, and *Don't mistreat people*. Paul Buchheit, Google's twenty-third employee, suggested *Don't be Evil*. Page and Brin adopted it as their corporate motto. They liked the idea that their company could be successful and make money, while still doing good things for the world.

With Google's growth came the expansion of the Googleplex campus, refurbished buildings, and the addition of vegetable gardens. Building 43 stood at the heart of the Googleplex, and became the main playground for engineers. Googlers met in rooms with exotic names like *Timbuktu* and *Mogadishu*. Bathrooms contained touch-pad controlled toilets with six levels of heat for the seats, automatic washing, drying, and flushing. Office cubicles contained huge flat-screen monitors.

Page and Brin worked in Office 211, a space filled with plants and computer monitors. The conference room next to their office had industrial gray carpeting, red velvet couches, large flat LCD screens, whiteboards, and projectors lining the gray walls. An exclusive meeting area above Page and Brin's office featured Astroturf carpet, a massage chair, and a whiteboard scribbled with projects and the words *Google's Master Plan*. Attracted by the buzz around Google, Page and Brin received distinguished visitors at the Googleplex, such as American presidents Jimmy Carter and Bill Clinton and vice president Al Gore.

"We run Google a little bit like a university," Brin told people. "We have lots of projects, about 100 of them. We like to have small groups of people, three or so people, working on projects. Some of them, for example, are related to molecular biology. Others involve building hardware. So we do lots of stuff. The only way you are going to have success is to have lots of failures first." In the casual atmosphere, new ideas emerged in offices, in the cafeteria, and at the gym. Some of the ideas launched new projects destined for worldwide use.

With Schmidt's supervision, Page and Brin were becoming savvier about finances and running a business. However, as Google continued to grow and to offer innovative technologies, the Google Guys faced many challenges. People also began to question whether the motto *Don't Be Evil* truly fit Page and Brin's company.

The Google Mail splash screen and logo

5

▶ By 2004, Page and Brin's company dominated search. Google was handling 100 million searches each day, approximately 1,000 searches per second. With more than 3,000 employees, Google continued to introduce new technologies to the world. The Google Guys decided to start offering their users an e-mail service.

Page and Brin wanted their e-mail to be the best on the Internet. They identified flaws in services offered by Microsoft, Yahoo!, and AOL. One problem with other services was that users often had difficulty finding older e-mails. Unable to store mountains of messages, AOL automatically deleted e-mails after thirty days.

Page and Brin launched Gmail in April 2004. With each e-mail account, they gave away one free gigabyte of storage on Google's network. Users also had the capability to search their old e-mails. At first, Page and Brin provided Gmail accounts to 1,000 people to test the service. These people could invite a limited number of friends to try Gmail. Page and Brin offered Gmail as an invitation-only service in order to discourage spammers from registering numerous accounts to send spam, or unwanted e-mails, to users.

One aspect of Gmail stirred up a firestorm, catching Page and Brin off guard. Gmail featured advertisements on one side of the page. Context words within the e-mails caused specific ads to appear. Users considered their e-mails to be personal and saw the ads as an invasion of their privacy. People grew concerned about Google employees reading their e-mails. But, "if we violate the privacy of our users, they'll leave us," Schmidt responded.

Politicians, privacy groups, and thousands of long-time Google users attacked Gmail. Numerous groups around the world wrote letters to Google demanding the suspension of Gmail. Columbia University professor Tim Wu summed up people's concerns, "Google, if it were a person, has all the flaws and all of the virtues of a classic Silicon Valley geek," he said. "In some ways, they are very principled. But they have this total deaf ear to certain types of issues. One of them is privacy. They just love that data because they can do neat things with it."

To sign up for a Gmail account, users needed to enter identifying information, such as name, address, telephone number, and sometimes credit card number. People worried about dishonest employees, lawyers, and private investigators sifting through the data Google retained, and the possibility of the government forcing Google to turn over sensitive information. Congressman John Dingell of Michigan called it a "virtual privacy time bomb." Although Google put privacy safeguards in place, people fretted about potential abuse.

"If you have something that you don't want anyone to know, maybe you shouldn't be doing it in the first place," Schmidt told users. "If you really need that kind of privacy, the reality is that search engines—including

The Gmail logo

Google—do retain this information for some time. . . . We're all subject in the U.S. to the Patriot Act and it is possible that that information could be made available to the authorities."

Despite the criticism, people wanted to try Gmail. Some sold their invitations on eBay, fetching up to $1,000. Page and Brin extended more invitations, and the buying and selling of Gmail invites slowed. As more people tried Gmail—and liked it—the criticism died down, although the controversy shook many users' confidence in Google and raised serious questions about online privacy.

Just weeks after the controversy over Gmail, Page and Brin revealed their plans to make Google a public company. Since 1998, Google had been privately owned, which offered advantages. Page and Brin didn't have to consider the needs of public investors or disclose their company's financial information. However, if Google became a public company, Page and

Brin's early, loyal employees could turn their stock, or shares in the company, into money; Page and Brin would become billionaires.

When a private company becomes a public company, its stock is sold to public investors during an initial public offering (IPO). Companies have many reasons for going public. An IPO can raise money to expand the business, pay debts, and make owners rich. Imagine a bakery losing money. Many people have stopped shopping there because they are allergic to nuts, and all cookies and cakes made at the bakery contain nuts or were made on equipment that processes nuts. The bakery's owners might hold an IPO to raise money for equipment and ingredients to make nut-free products.

Often a company's founders issue stock to early employees and private investors who funded the company as a reward for helping lay the foundation of the business. However, the shares have little value at first because the stock isn't publicly traded. After the IPO, shares can increase in value, sometimes by huge amounts. People who own many early shares can become very wealthy by selling their shares. Sometimes business owners want to get the company going, make it profitable, and then sell their shares and move on. Some don't want to run the business forever. Others just enjoy starting new companies.

IPOs also have drawbacks. Companies can spend thousands of dollars in fees associated with registering an IPO. They often hire experts to help them navigate the paperwork and complex rules of the Securities & Exchange Commission (SEC), the federal agency that regulates the U.S. stock market to prevent fraud.

The New York Stock Exchange on Wall Street

When a private company becomes public, the primary owners can no longer make independent decisions. The shareholders, or investors who purchased stock, now own a portion of the company, although they aren't involved in the day-to-day operations. SEC regulations require shareholder meetings and approval for certain decisions. Investors want the value of their stock to increase. If it decreases, they may sell their stock, which could impact the overall value of the company and drive it out of business.

Months of planning go into the IPO process. The cast of characters includes accountants, advisors, and investment bankers, called underwriters, who help set the initial offering price for the stock. The underwriter creates a prospectus, a document describing the company in detail to potential investors. On the day of the IPO, usually 80 percent of the stock is sold to large firms, investment banks, and high-profile investors. The stock price increases and decreases depending on the confidence in the company and the stock market.

Google's IPO caused a media sensation. The company's financial growth in the previous few years astounded people. Google's profits now equaled more than $100 million. Just as Page and Brin ran their company differently, they wanted their IPO to be different. They called their prospectus the *Letter from the Founders: An Owner's Manual for Google's Shareholders.* "Google is not a conventional company," wrote Page and Brin to investors. "We do not intend to become one." According to the prospectus, Page, Brin, and Schmidt would continue making all major decisions, not shareholders. Instead of allocating 80 percent of their stocks to be sold to large banking institutions, Page and Brin held an auction, in which anyone who wanted a share of Google stock could place a bid. It gave all investors—big and small—the same opportunity to invest in Google. The bids determined the initial price at which everyone got their shares. Google's stock was initially offered at eighty-five dollars per share on August 19, 2004. By the end of the first day, the stock had risen to one hundred dollars per share. Within months it doubled and within a year it stood at more than three hundred dollars per share.

Google's IPO, the largest and most successful technology IPO ever, raised almost $3 billion for the company. The IPO made instant millionaires of more than 1,000 Google employees who owned stock options. Page and Brin became the world's youngest self-made billionaires, each with an estimated worth of $7 to $10 billion. *Vanity Fair* magazine ranked them the most powerful leaders of the information age. They had no plans to retire soon though. "If we were motivated by money, we would have sold the company a long time ago and ended up on a beach," said Page.

However, on the heels of Page and Brin's lucrative IPO, Geico, an insurance company, sued Google. Geico objected to the way Google profited by selling ads to the insurance company's competition, using keywords linked to names trademarked by Geico. Other insurance companies could bid on the words *Geico* or *Geico Direct*. Geico claimed they were losing business because a competitor's ad could appear when a user typed in the search word *Geico*. Although rival companies could bid on the trademarked names, Google's policies prohibited them from using those names in the headlines of their ads. Page and Brin won the dispute when a judge ruled that Geico hadn't offered enough evidence to prove their case.

In this 2004 photo, a cameraman focuses his lens on the board at the Nasdaq Marketsite in New York shortly after shares of the Internet search engine giant started trading.

ADVANCES
1255
Total Issues Traded 2,897
NASDAQ
-0.1%
2846
NASDAQ
135.28
Google
+14.0%
NASDAQ Listed GOOG
NASDAQ
Microsoft
-0.9%
2722
9693
+1193
NASDAQ
1871
1831
1791

The year 2004 ended with several personal triumphs for Page and Brin. They both won the Marconi Prize, awarded annually to people who carry on the work of Guglielmo Marconi who pioneered achievements in wireless technology. The society recognized them for their contributions to human progress in information technology.

Page also was inducted into the National Academy of Engineering. He earned the prestigious award for helping develop innovative advances in technology and engineering. Soon afterwards, Brin also became a member of the academy.

In late December 2004, Page and Brin's company performed an important public service after a tsunami with fifty-foot-tall waves traveling at the speed of jet airplanes

A lone, partially destroyed house stands amid litter and debris on a street in downtown Banda Aceh in Indonesia, following the tsunami that struck the area in December 2004.

devastated Southeast Asia. In just one day, more than 150,000 people were killed and more than 1 million people in eleven countries became homeless. Page and Brin used Google's homepage to convey important messages and to provide links to international relief efforts. Both were proud of their ability to offer Google's services as a way of helping after a natural disaster.

Google had users and enthusiastic fans across the world. One couple even gave their baby the middle name Google. Soon Page and Brin expanded Google's services to China. In late 2005, the company reached an agreement with the Chinese government to provide services to more than 1 billion citizens in the People's Republic of China. However, Google agreed to only provide search results sanctioned by the restrictive Communist government. No information would appear about topics such as a 1989 uprising in China, during which the Chinese government massacred hundreds of pro-Democracy protesters. Many people questioned Google's decision. However, despite being censored, Page and Brin liked that Google's search results offered people in China a wealth of information previously unavailable to them.

Page and Brin were continuing to expand Google's borders. Many wondered where they would take the company next.

Queen Elizabeth at Google's United
Kingdom headquarters in London in 2008

6

▶ By 2006, Page and Brin stood atop one of America's richest corporations. The Google Guys wanted to use their company's vast financial resources and their employees' creativity and talent to do more. Hoping to make Google more than just a search engine, they founded Google.org to address worldwide problems. "Obviously everyone wants to be successful, but I want to be looked back on as being very innovative, very trusted and ethical and ultimately making a big difference in the world," said Brin. He and Page hired Dr. Larry Brilliant, a world health expert, to head up Google.org. A medical doctor, Brilliant had helped to eradicate smallpox in India in the 1970s. Google "does not want to be part of the problem; we want to be part of the solution," Brilliant said.

Larry Brilliant

Page and Brin wanted Google.org to focus on technology-driven philanthropy to do good across the planet—from preventing disease to developing more efficient, cheaper electric cars. The organization offered scholarships to students interested in technological fields and provided funding for innovative projects.

Google.org funded researchers who were attempting to better predict and prevent natural disasters. They also organized studies that examined factors impacting the spread of disease, such as climate change, international travel, and contact with animals. "What if we could have been there when the HIV [human immunodeficiency virus] moved from animal to chimp to human and [we] could have averted that risk?" said Brilliant. "To prevent or abort or slow a pandemic saves tens of millions of lives." In its first three years, Google.org spent up to $175 million.

One day, Page and Brin would institute the Project 10 to the 100th prize. They offered $10 million in prize money, to be divided among five organizations with the best world-changing ideas. Google received more than 150,000 suggestions and asked the public to vote for the top five ideas. It took 3,000 Googlers to review the ideas and one year to award the prize money. One of the winners was the group FIRST, an organization that works to get children and teenagers excited about science and technology though competitions like robot and Lego building.

Soon Page and Brin started another project. Hoping to combat the sea of incorrect information on the Internet, they wanted to make millions of books available online. "There is fantastic information in books," said Brin. "Often when I do a search, what is in a book is miles ahead of what I find on a Web site." Page and Brin dreamed of computer users—from kindergartners to college professors—being able to access full textbooks. Page and Brin hoped the project would provide people in developing countries with access to literature and information. "Google's mission is to organize the world's information and make it universally accessible and useful," Brin said. "The tremendous wealth of knowledge that lies within the books of the world will now be at their fingertips."

However, there were many hurdles to the project. Page and Brin needed to develop the technology to digitize books efficiently and accurately on a giant scale and to find libraries interested in the project. They also needed to address potential copyright issues.

Page traveled to the University of Michigan, where he offered that Google would foot the bill for scanning every book, nearly 7 million volumes, in the university's library.

Soon Stanford, Harvard, and Oxford also expressed interest in the digital book project. Google would be digitizing miles and miles of books and adding the information to its index. The database could potentially contain many millions of books.

Page and Brin looked into developing new scanning devices that would treat books gently. Flatbed scanner technology allowed people to scan one item at a time. A few years earlier, Page and Marissa Mayer, an early employee, had experimented with scanning books. The two turned the pages of a three hundred-page book one page at a time, ticking off the rhythm with a metronome. It took forty minutes. Now, Page and Brin tested robotic devices, using mechanical arms and suction to turn the pages. They decided to use an army of trained personnel and digital cameras that could snap images in a fraction of a second. But it wasn't technology that presented the biggest stumbling block to the project. It was copyright laws.

Copyright laws protect books, music, movies, video games, art work, computer programs, and other published works—whether online or in print. Laws protect the material from being copied and spread without the consent of the author, publisher, or third party. In 1709, Queen Anne of England decreed the Statute of Anne, one of the first copyright laws. It granted the exclusive right of publication to authors for twenty-one years. Today, copyright laws vary depending on when the work was produced. Page and Brin promised to respect copyright laws and to reimburse the libraries for any lawsuits over digitizing the books.

Soon Page and Brin unveiled Google Print. It covered the costs of digitizing the books in return for the right to display a snippet of text matching a query. Users would be unable to

Sergey Brin, left, and Larry Page at the Book Fair in Frankfurt, Germany, in October 2004

copy or print the information, but Google would provide links to Web sites selling the books. Page and Brin met with large publishing companies about supplying books to the project. Publishers could run ads on the pages with the displayed text. Like any other advertiser, they would pay based on the number of clicks the ads generated, and Google would share the ad revenue.

The Author's Guild and the Association of American Publishers sued Google over the project, arguing it was illegal to show portions of material still under copyright. Google countered it was no different than a card catalog in a library that offered a brief summary of the book. Google and the publishers eventually reached a compromise. Google would pay $125 million in exchange for the right to provide full text versions of out-of-print books.

Later in 2006, Page and Brin acquired other types of online technology. Google paid $1.6 billion to buy YouTube, a site on which people post homemade videos. YouTube's owners sold their site to Google because they couldn't keep up with the online traffic. The site had grown quickly, attracting millions of users. Page and Brin's users could now search keywords, images, videos, and music.

Larry Page and Sergey Brin appearing in a video link on the YouTube Web site. Google has acquired the online video sharing company.

Although many people still saw Google as a likeable and growing company, others disliked how Google ate into their markets. Advertising companies lost money when clients turned to Google. Telephone companies worried about Google entering the rapidly changing cell phone business.

In June 2007, Apple had introduced its iPhone, a product that revolutionized the cell phone and Internet industry. Apple's iPhone was the first cell phone with e-mail and Web browsing capability. Users could send e-mails and text messages, listen to music, and talk —all by using a touch screen and virtual keyboard. The iPhone suddenly made Internet users mobile, no longer tied to their computers. In three months, Apple sold more than 1.4 million iPhones, becoming the most valuable tech company in the world.

Many people awaited the unveiling of the gPhone, Google's answer to the iPhone. Instead of a phone, Page and Brin introduced a free cell phone software operating system called Android. The software could run on millions of devices around the world. With Android, Google sparked greater use of Internet-ready phones called *smartphones*. "This Google proposal can do to cell phones what the Internet did for the personal computer," said David Weinberger, a researcher at Harvard. "The Internet created a new public space, and the opening up of cell phones will do the same thing, but extend that space beyond the time that we spend tapping at a keyboard." Soon 160,000 new Android-enabled phones were being activated each day. Google had made a giant leap and taken their search capabilities mobile.

The year 2007 was eventful for Page and Brin in other ways. In May, Brin married Anne Wojcicki. The two met through Wojcicki's sister, Susan, who had rented her garage to Page and Brin in 1998. Both adventurous and outgoing, Brin and Wojcicki liked yoga, scuba diving, and kite surfing. She had attended Yale University and graduated with a degree in biology.

Brin and Wojcicki were married in the Bahamas on Musha Cay, an exclusive, private island ringed by sugar-white sand beaches and clear turquoise-blue waters. Wedding guests were flown in by private jet and ferried to a sandbar. Brin wore a tuxedo-black swimsuit and Wojcicki wore a wedding dress-white swimsuit. The two swam out to a sandbar where friends married them.

In December 2007, Page also wed. He married Lucy Southworth, a former model who was earning a PhD from Stanford. She had earned her master's degree in science from Oxford University and done medical social work in South Africa. The two had begun dating in 2006. Like Page, she was intelligent and quiet. Page and Southworth married on exotic, luxurious Necker Island in the Caribbean Sea.

Page and Brin strove to keep their personal lives private and rarely gave interviews. Despite their recent marriages, they continued to work long hours to develop new services. In addition to going mobile, the Internet was swiftly evolving in other ways. People increasingly went online for social interaction. In 2004, Mark Zuckerberg developed a site called

In 2011, Barack Obama speaks to Mark Zuckerberg before a private meeting where Obama dined with technology business leaders.

Facebook to help users communicate with their friends, family, and co-workers. Facebook users have home pages with personal profiles and news feeds of status updates from friends. By 2008, Facebook had 100 million users.

People also flocked to Twitter, a social networking and blogging site, launched in 2006. Twitter users post and read brief text-based messages, called tweets, about their activities. Like Facebook, Twitter use had increased by leaps and bounds.

For many years, people had gone to Google for answers to their questions. Now, increasingly popular social media sites encroached on Google's market. Instead of turning to Google to decide what bicycle to buy, people could ask friends on Facebook or Twitter. Or, they might visit the Web site Groupon, which offers coupons to groups, to find a bargain on, say, bikes or restaurants or spas.

Google's investors worried about the company's ability to keep up with the changing Internet. "It's a growing chink in their armor," said a former Googler. "They know that. The question is, what can they do about it?" Page and Brin continued to search for ways to create their own social media approaches, such as Google sites, a Web site dedicated to bringing users with common interests together.

Now with seventy offices throughout the world—from Texas to Turkey, Google had more than 23,000 employees and revenue of $20 billion a year. Google's services stretched like

The Google Engineering Center in Zurich, Switzerland

a web across the planet. The word *Google* even appeared in dictionaries. The British newspaper the *Guardian* named Page and Brin the two most influential individuals in the media. Others called them the "the "princes of high technology," and the "lords of all information." The business Page and Brin had started in a garage was now the world's second most valuable technology company after Microsoft.

Larry Page speaks at WIRED NextFest in Los Angeles in September 2007, presenting the Google Lunar X PRIZE.

7

To the Moon and Beyond

In April 2011, Page replaced Eric Schmidt as the company's CEO. Schmidt, set to continue as the chairman of the board of directors and to serve as Google's executive chairman, tweeted of the change: "Day-to-day adult supervision no longer needed!" In an official Google blog, he added, "Larry, in my clear opinion, is ready to lead."

Both Page and Brin want to keep inventing and to see how much more they can change the world. Their base remains the Googleplex—home to scientists, engineers, statisticians, product marketers, and former CEOs. Employees thread their way between the main buildings on cobbled paths and use a zipline between two buildings separated by a small creek. Massive stone statues of explorers like Jacques Cousteau dot the pathways. On sunny days, Googlers enjoy their healthy, free meals at outside tables. They can stroll through the vegetable garden or stop by the Hiveplex, an area with four beehives painted in Google's colors, where the company harvests its own honey. A bronze replica of a Tyrannosaurus Rex, nicknamed Stan, guards the main building. Although the Googleplex resembles a playground, Googlers are dedicated to their work. "Ambition is a very important part of our culture," said Brin, "and the depth of science you can do at Google is [like] nowhere else in the world."

Google's innovation continues to change the world, having evolved far beyond simple, better search. Early in 2011, people turned to Google's new PeopleFinder service to search for missing family members and friends following a devastating earthquake and tsunami in Japan. Users also can now explore services like Google Earth, Google Maps, Google Finance, Google Calendar, Google Desktop, Gmail, Google Documents, and Google's new lightening-fast browser called Chrome. The company handles more than 1 billion searches each day. Two of every three online queries involve Google's search engine. Their index contains an estimated 25.2 billion Web pages. Android phones hold 26 percent of the market and Google is developing its own library of apps, or mini programs ranging from translators and flashlights to entertaining.

Page's and Brin's innovative approaches still bring criticism though. People continue to say Google violates their privacy and uses others' intellectual property both on Google News and by digitizing books. "We do run into a lot of areas where our innovation bumps up against laws that were not designed for the world we now live in," said David Drummond, a Google lawyer. "Sometimes others don't share our commitment [to change]." However, Google continues the process of digitizing millions of books hoping to tear down the physical limits of libraries.

Page and Brin had hoped to break down the walls of censorship in China. However, when they learned of Chinese leaders ordering attempts to hack into Google's networks, they threatened to leave China unless the government allowed them to run an uncensored search engine. When officials refused, Google pulled out of China, redirecting search traffic to their uncensored site in Hong Kong.

Google's China headquarters in Tsinghua Science Park, Beijing, China

Recently, Page and Brin have turned their attention to another critical issue—their energy consumption. Google uses massive amounts of energy to maintain its super network of "server farms" that are scattered from Atlanta to Zurich. Although the number of computers Google uses is kept secret, experts estimate the number to be more than 1 million. Page and Brin have begun using clean, renewable energy. They installed solar panels on the roofs of the buildings in the Googleplex and invested $39 million in wind power. When dry brush in the fields near their headquarters became a fire hazard, they rented goats to help trim the grass in a low-carbon way.

Page and Brin also installed solar-powered stations in their company's parking lots to charge their fleet of hybrid cars. Both Page and Brin drive electric cars produced by Tesla Motors. Named after the scientist Tesla, the company builds the world's fastest and most energy-efficient cars. A Tesla sports car can travel up to 130 miles per hour and go 250 miles on a single battery charge.

The 2009 Tesla Roadster

Page and Brin also are looking to the moon as a stepping stone to the rest of the universe. By exploring the moon, scientists can study whether the clean, solar energy in space could be used on Earth. Page and Brin have announced their plans for the Google Lunar X PRIZE. The program offers $30 million in prizes, challenging teams of engineers and entrepreneurs from around the world to design the best robotic moon rovers. Google's founders hope the technological advances the prize inspires will one day improve life on Earth. Brin also has invested in Space Adventures, a company offering opportunities for private spaceflight. Brin's investment helped fund the program and reserved him a spot on a future mission orbiting the moon.

Page and Brin have also started using Google's resources to pioneer breakthroughs in medicine and health. Genetics research especially interests Brin, who discovered he has a 50 percent risk of developing Parkinson's disease. He has begun spending millions to research the disease, from which his mother Eugenia suffers.

Parkinson's is an incurable brain condition that progressively worsens. People with Parkinson's disease experience tremors, slowness and stiffness when moving, and impaired balance. The disease is caused by the death of brain cells that are responsible for making

Dr. Buzz Aldrin, right, an Apollo astronaut, responds to a question during a presentation of the $30 million Lunar X PRIZE. Also pictured are Bob Weiss, left, vice-chairman of the X PRIZE Foundation, Larry Page, second from left, and Dr. Peter Diamondis, the chairman and chief executive officer of X PRIZE Foundation.

and releasing a chemical in the brain called dopamine. What starts the process is unknown. Medications can help relieve the symptoms, but no known cure exists.

Brin has started a program that offers Parkinson's patients the opportunity to have their DNA analyzed through his wife's genetic research company 23andMe. The information can be used to investigate genetic and environmental factors in the hopes of advancing treatment. "Individually, our genes and experiences are lost in a sea of statistical noise," Brin said. "But, taken together they become a high power lens on our inner workings."

Google continues to dominate the Internet and mobile phone world. Users can wake up with an alarm set on their Google Android phone, read about world events on Google News, check Gmail for new e-mails, use Google Maps to get to a store, visit Google Groups or Blogger to see what friends are doing, stay organized on their Google Calendars, and watch entertaining videos on YouTube.

Some people compare the creation of Google to the invention of the printing press in the 1440s by Johaness Gutenberg. Gutenberg was the first to create moveable metal type pieces to use in a printing press. His lettered pieces could be assembled and disassembled to print different words. Gutenberg's invention launched the modern printing press, making books more affordable and available to the masses. Like Gutenberg's invention, Google provides greater access to information.

Despite the criticism the Google Guys have faced, they continue pushing the edge of the envelope and developing innovative technologies to improve the world. Having earned fame and fortune, they stand at the head of a company that has won at least twenty-two Webby Awards and more than one hundred awards from newspapers, magazines, universities, and other institutions.

"They were groomed for greatness in the computer field from infancy; they traveled to a holy land (Stanford University and Silicon Valley) to prove their mettle in battle," said author Janet Lowe. "They slew a whole den of dragons and emerged from the quest with flags of victory flying. Their story is a classic hero's journey."

In 1998, Larry Page and Sergey Brin had sadly packed up their things when they left Stanford. From that small, dilapidated garage near the university, the two could hardly have foreseen their company becoming an international phenomenon.

"Two kind of crazy kids have had a big impact on the world because of the power of the Internet, the power of the distribution, and the power of software and computers," Page said. "And there are so many things like that out there. There are so many opportunities where you can have a huge impact on the world by using the leverage of science and technology."

Themed Google logos

Timeline

1973	Larry Page born on March 26 in East Lansing, Michigan; Sergey Brin born on August 21 in Moscow, Russia.
1979	The Brins immigrate to the United States; Page gets his first computer.
1982	Brin receives a computer for his birthday.
1995	Page and Brin meet at Stanford University.
1996	Develop PageRank technology and a search engine named BackRub.
1997	Change BackRub's name to Google.
1998	Leave Stanford and form Google, Inc. on September 4.
1999	Move from their garage headquarters to new location in Mountain View.
2000	Win their first Webby Award in May; launch AdWords.
2001	Hire Eric Schmidt as CEO; open first international office; launch Google Images.
2002	Introduce Google News; begin partnering with sites for new search box program.
2004	Become billionaires after Google's IPO; move to the Googleplex; win the Marconi Prize; inducted into the National Academy of Engineering.
2005	Google Maps and Blogger go live.
2006	Start Google.org; begin the digital books project; acquire YouTube.
2007	Brin marries Anne Wojcicki; Page marries Lucy Southworth; introduce Android.
2008	Celebrate Google's tenth anniversary; digitize millions of magazine articles.
2009	Organize first YouTube symphony orchestra; introduce All For Good to help volunteers find local opportunities.
2010	Stop providing censored search results in China; make Google Street View available for all seven continents.
2011	Page becomes CEO; Google Earth helps locate victims after tsunami in Japan.

Sources

CHAPTER 1: The Boys Who Loved Computers

p. 10,   "the Swiss Army knife . . ." David A. Vise and Mark Malseed,
          The Google Story (New York: Delacorte Press, 2005), 144.

p. 10,   "I think it . . ." Vise and Malseed, *The Google Story*, 16.

p. 14,   "He said he wouldn't . . ." Mark Malseed, "The Story of Sergey Brin," *Moment*,
          February 2009, http://www.momentmag.com.

p. 15,   "We were in . . ." Ibid.

p. 15,   "The U.S. was . . ." Richard L. Brandt, *Inside Larry and Sergey's Brain*
          (New York: Portfolio, 2009), 28.

p. 20,   "It's a very . . ." John Battelle, *The Search: How Google and Its Rivals Rewrote
          the Rules of Business and Transformed Our Culture* (New York: Portfolio,
          2005), 66.

p. 20,   "Sergey was . . ." Janet Lowe, *Google Speaks: Secrets of the World's Greatest
          Billionaire Entrepreneurs, Sergey Brin and Larry Page*, 13.

p. 20,   "He was a . . ." Ibid, 16.

p. 21,   "Almost half the . . ." Vise and Malseed, *The Google Story*, 28.

p. 22,   "Is it true . . ." Malseed, "The Story of Sergey Brin."

CHAPTER 2: "LarryandSergey"

p. 26,   "We both found . . ." Battelle, *The Search: How Google and Its Rivals
          Rewrote the Rules of Business and Transformed Our Culture*, 68.

p. 26,   "They were both . . ." Vise and Malseed, *The Google Story*, 34.

p. 26,   "two swords sharpening . . ." Ken Auletta, *Googled: The End of the World
          as We Know It* (New York, The Penguin Press, 2009), 38.

p. 27,   "I expected him . . ." Vise and Malseed, *The Google Story*, 28.

p. 27,   "I tried so many . . ." Ibid, 29.

p. 30,   "I was hoping . . ." Adi Ignatius, "Meet the Google Guys," *Time*,
          February 12, 2006, http://www.time.com.

p. 31,   "Search was not pretty . . ." Vise and Malseed, *The Google Story*, 35.

p. 33,   "The perfect search engine . . ." "Ten Things We Know To Be True,"
          Google, http://www.google.com.

p. 34,   "We were confused . . ." Vise and Malseed, *The Google Story*, 17.

p. 34,   "We sat around . . ." Ibid, 12.

p. 34,   "snarfed a whole . . ." Randall Stross, *Planet Google: One Company's
          Audacious Plan to Organize Everything We Know* (New York: Free Press,
          2008), 50.

p. 35,   "They were excited . . ." Vise and Malseed, *The Google Story*, 41.

p. 36,   "Other Web sites took . . ." Ibid, 47.

p. 36,   "We were definitely . . ." Malseed, "The Story of Sergey Brin."

CHAPTER 3: From Garage to Googleplex

p. 40, "I fear someone . . ." Auletta, *Googled: The End of the World as We Know It*, 28.

pp. 40-41, "It was important . . ." Yuval Saar, "The Israeli Woman Behind the Google Logo," *Haaretz*, February 11, 2008, http://www.haaretz.com.

p. 42, "To just invent something . . ." Vise and Malseed, *The Google Story*, 18.

p. 45, "garden-variety PCs . . ." Ibid, 3.

p. 47, "I don't think . . ." Ibid.

p. 50, "Competition is a good . . ." Lowe, *Google Speaks: Secrets of the World's Greatest Billionaire Entrepreneurs, Sergey Brin and Larry Page*, 272.

p. 52, "We love you . . ." "Google Wins Webby and People's Voice Awards for Best Technical Achievement," Google, May 12, 2000, http://www.google.com.

p. 52, "Google's new gigantic index . . ." "Google Launches World's Largest Search Engine," Google, June 26, 2000, http://www.google.com.

CHAPTER 4: Google Grows

p. 57, "They thought everyone . . ." Auletta, *Googled: The End of the World as We Know It*, 64.

p. 57, "day-to-day adult supervision . . ." Michael Liedtke, "Google Cofounder Page to Replace Schmidt as CEO," Yahoo! News, January 20, 2011, http://www.yahoo.com.

p. 58, "They resisted hiring . . ." Auletta, *Googled: The End of the World as We Know It*, 64.

p. 65, "We run Google . . ." Vise and Malseed, *The Google Story*, 16.

CHAPTER 5: Ups and Downs

p. 68, "if we violate . . ."Auletta, *Googled: The End of the World as We Know It*, 198.

p. 68, "Google, if it were . . ." Ibid, 198.

p. 69, "virtual privacy time bomb . . ." Abbey Klaassen, "Google-DoubleClick Tie-Up Faces Congress," *Crain's New York*, July 17, 2007, http://www.crainsnewyork.com.

p. 69, "If you have . . ." "Google CEO on Privacy," December 7, 2009, *Huffington Post*, http://www.huffingtonpost.com.

p. 72, "Google is not . . ." "How Long Will Google's Magic Last?" *Economist*, December 4, 2010, http://www.economist.com.

p. 73, "If we were . . ." Ignatius, "Meet the Google Guys."

CHAPTER 6: Changing the World

p. 79,   "Obviously everyone wants . . ." "Persons of the Week: Larry Page and Sergey Brin," ABC News, February 20, 2011, http://www.abcnews.go.com.

p. 79,   "does not want . . ." Harriet Rubin, "Google Offers a Map for its Philanthropy," *New York Times*, January 18, 2008, http://www.nytimes.com.

p. 80,   "What if we . . ." Ibid.

p. 81,   "There is fantastic . . ." Brandt, *Inside Larry and Sergey's Brain*, 167.

p. 81,   "Google's mission is . . ." Ibid, 168.

p. 85,   "This Google proposal . . ." Chris Gaylord, "Hurdles Ahead for Google's Cell Phone Plan," *Christian Science Monitor*, November 8, 2007, http://www.csmonitor.com.

p. 88,   "It's a growing chink . . ." Michael V. Copeland and Seth Weintraub, "Google: The Search Party is Over," *Fortune International*, August 16, 2010, http://www.tech.fortune.cnn.com.

p. 89,   "Princes of High Technology . . ." Lowe, *Google Speaks: Secrets of the World's Greatest Billionaire Entrepreneurs, Sergey Brin and Larry Page*, 2.

CHAPTER 7: To the Moon and Beyond

p. 91,   "Day-to-day adult supervision . . ." Amy Lee, "Meet Larry Page, Google's New CEO," *Huffington Post*, Janary 21, 2011, http://www.huffingtonpost.com/2011/01/20/larry-page-google-ceo_n_811930.html.

p. 91,   "Larry, in my clear . . ." Ibid.

p. 91,   "Google's ambition is . . ." Lowe, *Google Speaks: Secrets of the World's Greatest Billionaire Entrepreneurs, Sergey Brin and Larry Page*, 132.

p. 92,   "Ambition is a very . . ." "How Long Will Google's Magic Last?" *Economist*.

p. 92,   "We do run into . . ." Brandt, *Inside Larry and Sergey's Brain*, 166.

p. 98,   "Individually, our genes . . ." Mark Henderson, "Google Founder Sergey Brin Pays for Parkinson's Gene Trial," *Times*, March 12, 2009, http://www.timesonline.co.uk.

p. 99,   "They were groomed . . ." Lowe, *Google Speaks: Secrets of the World's Greatest Billionaire Entrepreneurs, Sergey Brin and Larry Page*, 2.

p. 99,   "Two kind of crazy . . ." Vise and Malseed, *The Google Story*, 13.

Bibliography

Albanesius, Chloe. "Google Unveils Google TV with Sony, Logitech, Intel as Partners." *PC Magazine*, May 20, 2010. http://www.pcmag.com.

Android official Web site. http://www.android.com.

Auletta, Ken. *Googled: The End of the World as We Know It*. New York: The Penguin Press, 2009.

Batelle, John. *The Search: How Google and Its Rivals Rewrote the Rules of Business and Transformed Our Culture*. New York: Portfolio, 2005.

Bennett, Drake. "Stopping Google." *Boston Globe*, June 22, 2008. http://www.bostonglobe.com.

Brandt, Richard L. *Inside Larry & Sergey's Brain*. New York: Portfolio, 2009.

Computer History Museum official Web site. http://www.computerhistory.org.

Copeland, Michael V., and Seth Weintraub. "Google: The Search Party is Over." *Fortune International*, August 16, 2010.

Federal Communications Commission official Web site. http://www.fcc.gov.

Gaylord, Chris. "Hurdles Ahead for Google's Cellphone Plan." *Christian Science Monitor*, November 8, 2007. http://www.csmonitor.com.

Goodman, Leah McGrath. "Married to the Google Billionaire." *Marie Claire*. http://www.marieclaire.com.

"Google CEO On Privacy." *Huffington Post*, December 7, 2009. http://www.huffingtonpost.com.

Google official Web site. http://www.google.com/about.html.

Hardy, Quentin. "When Google Runs Your Life." *Forbes*, December 28, 2009.

Henderson, Max. "Google Founder Sergey Brin Pays for Parkinson's Gene Trial." *Times*, March 12, 2009. http://www.timesonline.co.uk.

Hirschorn, Michael. "The Digital Frontier." *Atlantic Monthly*, July/August 2010.

"How Long Will Google's Magic Last?" *Economist*, December 4, 2010.

Ignatius, Adi. "Meet The Google Guys." *Time*, February 12, 2006. http://www.time.com.

Jefferson, Graham. "Apple and Google Square Off." *USA Today*, June 7, 2010.

Jennings, Peter. "Persons of the Week: Larry Page and Sergey Brin." *ABC News*, February 20, 2011. http://www.abcnews.go.com.

Klaassen, Abbey. "Google-DoubleClick Tie-Up Faces Congress." *Crain's New York*, July 17, 2007. http://www.crainsnewyork.com.

Krazit, Tom. "Google Announces Project 10 to the 100th Themes." CNet News, September 24, 2009. http://www.news.cnet.com.

Liedtke, Michael. "Google Co-Founder Page to Replace Schmidt as CEO." Yahoo! News, January 20, 2011. http://www.news.yahoo.com.

Lombardi, Candace. "Google Joins Xerox as a Word." CNet News, July 6, 2006. http://www.news.cnet.com.

Lowe, Janet. *Google Speaks: Secrets of the World's Greatest Billionaire Entrepreneurs, Sergey Brin and Larry Page*. Hoboken, New Jersey: John Wiley & Sons, Inc., 2009.

Malseed, Mark. "The Story of Sergey Brin." *Moment*, February 2007. http://www.momentmag.com.

Nakashima, Ellen. "Chinese Leaders Ordered Google Hack, US Cable Quotes Source as Saying." *Washington Post*, December 4, 2010. http://washingtonpost.com.

Polastron, Lucien. *The Great Digitization and the Quest to Know Everything*. Rochester, Vermont: Inner Traditions, 2009.

Rubin, Harriet. "Google Offers a Map for its Philanthropy." *New York Times*, January 18, 2008. http://www.nytimes.com.

Saar, Yuval. "The Israeli Woman Behind the Google Logo." *Haaretz Daily Newspaper*, February 11, 2008. http://www.haaretz.com.

"Spotlight: Larry Page." *Star*, January 24, 2011. http://www.star.com.

Stross, Randall. *Planet Google: One Company's Audacious Plan to Organize Everything We Know*. New York: Free Press, 2008.

Vise, David A., and Mark Malseed. *The Google Story*. New York: Delacorte Press, 2005.

Wearden, Graeme. "Google Cofounder Weds." *Guardian*, December 10, 2007. http://www.guardian.co.uk.

Webby Awards official Web site. http://www.Webbyawards.com.

"The World: The Soviet Union: The Risks of Reform." *Time*, March 29, 1971. http://www.time.com.

Web sites

http://www.google.com

The official Google Web site features an "About Google" button that provides in-depth information about the company's services, pictures of Google Doodles, and blogs from Googlers, along with recent news and a history of the company.

http://www.google.org

This is the official Web site of Google's charitable foundation. It offers news about the company's high-tech projects that address global issues and a link to find volunteer opportunities near you.

http://www.computerhistory.org

Readers interested in learning more about computers can find information on this site, as well as view online exhibitions featuring pictures and descriptions of key events in computer history.

Index

Photo Credits

Cover: AP Photo/Ben Margot
4-5:   AP Photo/Uwe Lein, file
7:              Used under license from iStockphoto.com
8:              AP Photo/Ben Margot
9:              Used under license from iStockphoto.com
11:             Used under license from iStockphoto.com
12:             Used under license from iStockphoto.com
15:             Used under license from iStockphoto.com
17:             Courtesy of the U.S. Army
18:             Courtesy of Rama
20-21:   Courtesy of Bill Bertram Boffy b
21:             Courtesy of Boffy b
22:             Courtesy of the National Science Foundation
24:             Courtesy of Jawed Karim
25:             Used under license from iStockphoto.com
28-29:   Courtesy of Elf
30:             Used under license from iStockphoto.com
35:             Courtesy of Mitchell Aidelbaum
38:             AP Photo/Marcio Jose Sanchez
39:             Used under license from iStockphoto.com
40:             Courtesy of Kees de Vos
44:             sjscreens / Alamy
46:             Courtesy of Steve Jurvetson
48-49:   AP Photo/Randi Lynn Beach
54:             Studioshots / Alamy
55:             Used under license from iStockphoto.com
58:             Courtesy of Charles Haynes
60:             Courtesy of Library of Congress
62-63:   Alex Segre / Alamy
66:             ICP / Alamy
67:             Used under license from iStockphoto.com
69:             PhotoEdit / Alamy
71:             Courtesy of Arnoldius
74-75:   AP Photo/Kathy Willens, file
76:             Courtesy of U.S. Department of Defense
78:             AP Photo/Adrian Dennis, pool
79:             Used under license from iStockphoto.com
80:             Courtesy of Robert Scoble
83:             Alexander R sche/dpa /Landov
84:             ROB KIM/Landov
87:             Courtesy of the White House
88:             AP Photo/Keystone, Walter Bieri, file
90:             AP Photo/Ric Francis
91:             Used under license from iStockphoto.com
93:             Lou Linwei / Alamy
94-95:   Drive Images / Alamy
96-97:   AP Photo/Ric Francis
100:            Emilio Ereza / Alamy